TO THE OCCUPIER

To The Occupier

Paul Demuth

© Copyright 2009. First published by:
Anaconda Editions
143 Lordship Lane
London SE22 8HX
email: editions@anacondaeditions.com

The right of Paul Demuth to be identified as the author of this work has been asserted by him in accordance with the Copyright, Designs and Patents Act 1988.

Cover illustration "View" by Covadonga Valdés

Cover design by Olga Fedina

A CIP catalogue record for this book is available from the British Library

ISBN 978 1 901990 03 4

Contents

THE ANTIQUE CHAIR

Wails of anguish emanate
From Manor Lodge.

Despite the prohibitive ribbon,
The antique chair's been spoilt.

The frame, it now transpires,
Was stained with coffee or smoke

To contrive the appearance
Of use and age.

But, keen to show initiative
And ingenuity,

The lady who comes to clean
Applied a toothbrush to each boss and groove,

And when she finished with it,
It looked as good as new.

THE RETURN

Funny, isn't it, she said,
gazing at the entrance,

how things look bigger through a small child's eyes.

A tree had caught his attention.
His eye had climbed
the horny, plated trunk

up to the swarm of prickly leaves

molesting a flat
on the third floor.

*But apart from that sense
of shrinkage*, she continued,

nothing's changed at all... except...

She pondered for a while
and looked around.

*I'm sure there was a plant here.
A nasty one that used to scratch my arms.*

SIDE BY SIDE

a woman,
her mascara
smudged across her cheek,
and a man

side by side
in a car

she says they never speak
he turns the radio up
to drown the windscreen-wipers' squeak

the music is exquisite
the strings succumb, with poise,
to a superb lament

and without that noise
the wipers, creating transparency,
have a lovely, graceful sweep
as they cast aside the rain
& occasional leaf

THAT POEM TO YOU

when i finished writing that poem to you
i folded it in two
put it on the vent
above the steering-wheel
placed my glasses on it
and stepped out

Returning later on,
I switched the heater on
and when I put my glasses on
that poem started fluttering
half-way up the wind-screen
beating the air
with its white wings

PARKED

That car was parked
beside that tree
by an old man.
I remember him walking off
through thickening flakes of snow.

The tyres are now all flat.
White blossoms deck the bonnet, roof & boot.
The ventilator is choked
with dark brown leaves.
On the passenger seat, a map.

THE DREAM

Awoken by the latch,
she stares through the bedroom window
until the crunch and pop
of gravel dies,

and then returns to bed.

At 6am
she's re-awoken by the alarm.

As she washes and dresses
and cleans her teeth,
she's haunted by a fragment of a dream,

the Venus by the drive,
illuminated by the Volvo's beam,
amid the blackness of the night.

Then, going out to work, she taps
on the spare room's door
to wake him up.

The usual groan
does not ensue,
so she opens the door and scans

the bed,
the floor,
the walls.

THE NEIGHBOUR

The blonde next door,
who owns a cat,
ignores me as a rule,

unless she's banging on the wall
when I put music on.

She lovingly calls
and croons my name
across the back-gardens each evening,
tapping a dish with a spoon.

TO THE OCCUPIER

This morning, going out to work,
I found a letter by the door
in the shared hall,
addressed to the Occupier of 64.

Neither A nor B were specified,
so I left it lying on the floor
and found it again this evening
leaning, unopened, against the wall.

JUNE

In the toilet
a mosquito,
its horn sawing the dark.

Back in the bedroom
the same note.
When I open the window it swells.

It throbs throughout the street.
Rubbing my leg, I speculate.
A pipe? A drill?

SUNDAY

She lies on her belly, naked,
as the bells of the Sacred Heart resound,
her legs together, straight.

From sacrum to big toes a cleavage runs,
dividing buttocks, thighs, calves, ankles, soles.
It's intersected by a second line,
the crease along the bottom's lower verge,

completing the figure of a cross
which, kneeling, he bends to kiss.

THE CALL

The scent of blossoms floats
through the window where he stands
gazing at the moon
ascending the darkening sky

Can you hear the birds? he asks
and holds the phone outside

Dazzled by the climbing sun,
she doesn't see the yellow leaves
beyond the pane,
but sees their shadows falling down her gown

and, as he speaks, she hears
the bellbird's call

DUNEDIN

City of Otago,
whose rivers, creeks
and lakes

supplied your wealth,
you're wet and bright.
These summer days

(without the patronage
your varsity supplies)
your shops & bars are quiet.

City built with gold,
above your spires
a rainbow glows.

NOT ALONE

i came away from the dance floor
and, as the drug began to take effect,
i sat among the tables by the bar

where i started to worry
that, in the wake of dunblane,
people might be wary
of a solitary man

but when i looked round to see
if people were looking at me
i learnt, with some relief,
that i wasn't, in fact, alone:

everyone was on their own

13

TOO LATE

Returning from a trip
to Paris, where he'd planned to meet Yvette,

he finds a card
among his mail,
cancelling the rendezvous.

When he was small,
his parents had a calendar
in which that very picture featured too.

Joy, serenity & love
could be mechanically induced

by gazing at the dove
cradled in the palms
of the white-gowned child;

but when they moved
to another house
the calendar disappeared.

Oblivious of the picture's fame,
he rued the loss
for years.

Now he's found it again
on a card that arrived too late.

INVIGILATION

I'm invigilating a Maths exam
with a colleague
in the Art Room.

The windows behind me are open
to introduce a breeze,
which means the broody cooing in the trees
is clearly audible.

Beside me, on the wall,
there is a reproduction of
Child With A Dove.

Facing me across the rows
of shoulders and prostrated backs,
my colleague mimes the aiming of a gun.

I plead for clemency
by pointing at the palm-cupped dove,
hoping it will soften her heart,
but as she mimes the blast
and blows away the smoke
a silence plummets through the air.

MEDIA STUDIES

I asked 9Y,
my remedial group,
to select some adverts
which they thought were misleading.

Andrew chose one with a stereo
towering like a monument
over a street of dancers.

He said it was misleading
because it made people look small.

LONDON BRIDGE

I'm doing Josie's buttons up
before we cross the Thames,
and she is begging me to hide
her doll *immediately*.

She says it looks too babyish.
Apparently some children in a bus
have indicated that they're unimpressed.

Because my bomber-jacket is too tight
for Pamela and me to share,
I make a sacrifice.

As we step into the blast
of that callous, Russian wind,
with my jacket rolled up under my arm,

and lurch towards the City,

a check-point looms
at the other end.

Policemen with submachine-guns
are checking peoples' things.

MARCH 94

A wall lined with a mirror and
a window
converge to make a corner in this room,

creating the illusion of
twin windows, side by side.
A news-stand in the street reports

that in the House of Death
another body has been found.
Pedestrians pass

behind the jamb
between the two adjacent panes
and fail to reappear.

THE LODGER

Leo, the lodger,
Suddenly had to leave.

He used to entertain the little girl
By cracking walnuts in his hand

Or lifting the front of the car
Off the ground,

So when she heard he'd left,
She was dismayed.

The day he left
Her father sobbed for hours.
He seemed to be appallingly bereft.

It saddened her
And she was confused.

Her mother and Leo
Had always got on.
They were always having a joke.

But she'd never had any idea
That her father was
So fond
Of him.

CLOSED ACCOUNT

I went to close our joint account.
A personal consultant took the card
with which we guaranteed our cheques.
Then she rooted through her drawer
and found some manicure scissors.
Fitting her filed and varnished nails
into the loops of steel,
she chatted to a colleague
at the adjacent desk,
and I watched the little blades
divide the plastic in two.

THE CORRESPONDENT

Microphone in one hand,
clip-board in the other,

the correspondent
is reporting from the deck

of a carrier in the Gulf.
Her face is slowly narrowing,

encroached from East & West
by hair blown by a Harrier.

After an unflinching display
of brinkmanship,

she finally has to act,
before her eyes are both submerged,

and risks a toss of the head.
Each iris circles its socket,

as her arms, temples and ears
are all of a sudden revealed

and her brow is surmounted
by a vertical blond shaft.

DONALD'S DEN

Hard for motorists to spot,
Donald's Den, a little toy-shop, squats
at the bottom of a paved incline.

 December is upon us and all day
Father Christmas paces the kerb
along a double yellow line.
He bears a placard:

    COME TO DONALD'S DEN!

Children wave adoringly
from the back-windows
of vanishing cars,
and a cold wind blows.

THE AIM IN 1984

This evening
on the box,
mr lawson says

the aim
of the cuts
is to stimulate the growth
of individual initiative.
It's, basically, a pruning job.

I stroll down the road
to buy some tobacco.

In the news-agent's window
there are several little ads.

One type, in particular,
is beginning to proliferate:

FRENCH LESSONS WITH BRIGITTE
(bordered with X's and little red hearts).

It seems that mr lawson's
methods are yielding fruit.

THE STORM

The rattle of pelted steel,
amid the sudden storm,
announced the arrival of the 12,

bearing her distant destination's name
and overtaking her.
She quickened her pace

as much as her baggage allowed
and, panting, reached
the sheltered stop

before the 12 had left.
Eventually it pulled away
and she waited under the drumming roof.

THE LIMP

Coldharbour Lane.
A woman with a limp.
A trainer on one foot.
On the other a high-heeled boot.

186 COLDHARBOUR LANE

Approaching with a hand-written CV,
you see the waving of a hand
recorded all over the pane.

On the awning
a letter has come unstitched.
It now says STATE AGENT.

Eyes to whitewashed glass, you see
that the inside has been stripped

though on the door the sign remains:

    TYPING SERVICE
    ALSO AVAILABLE

THE MONSTER

I passed a group of teenage boys today
as I wheeled the baby
out of the playground.

They asked me for a light.

When I approached, I had a shock.

From mime & broken English I inferred:

> *war...*
> *wounds...*
> *a clinic in the area...*

And, walking home, I suddenly
remembered what my crazy neighbour said.

Last night when she was strolling past the park
she thought she saw a monster
with a head like shapeless, molten wax,
staggering towards her in the dark.

THE BOOK

I find my page,
whose corner I unbend.

As a rumble, to my left,
grows into a roar,

the pages I have read start fidgeting.
One by one they flip

over to the right-hand side
until the frontispiece

is lidded by the cover with a clap.
Ahead of me

a pair of sliding doors
divide.

HOOP ANCHOR TOP EGG

one morning, on the tube,
Josie named each letter she saw
after the things they stand for
in her alphabet picture book

a man with a letter tattooed
on each finger of each hand
sat beside us, slumbering

Hoop, she began.
Anchor. Top. Egg

That's very good, I said.
Soon you'll be able to read

BODY HEAT

She asked for Moody Thing
(the kitten with a pout),
which I rolled up and bound
with a rubber band.

Taking it, she said
that as an after-thought
she also wanted Body Heat
(the three male steaming nudes).

Laminated? I enquired.
Yeah, with the condom on someone advised.
I rolled it up
and, running out of bands,

I pushed it up inside
the first one she had bought
which, legs astride,
she steadied with both hands.

THAT SORT OF THING

A woman in Romford asked
for Number 17.
Locating it in my stock-case,
I saw it was the female nude
mounted on a bike.

It's for my boyfriend she explained.
He likes that sort of thing

In Bromley, on the other hand,
a man requested 21.
Extracting it from the case,
I saw it was the three male nudes,
languishing in a Turkish bath.

It's for my girlfriend he explained.
She likes that sort of thing

POSTERS

in the pedestrian zone
of the new town
i taped the display-sheet
to the ground

and created an island
in the cross-current
of shoppers, which slowed and hardened
like the setting round a jewel
as the images attracted countless souls

though not the man
wearing shades
escorted by a labrador
& equipped with a white cane

who left the prints
of his wellington boots

all over Dolphin World
Mona Lisa smoking dope
Without Stress Life Would Be Empty
& the tiger with glass eyes

THE NEWS (1984)

beside me on the tube
a man is reading a paper
a paper he has bought

i peer discreetly
and read, free of charge,

>   *a new*
> *democracy*
>   *of property-*
> *owners*

a dent in the page
obscures the rest

i crane my neck
but fail to evade
his radar

and he snatches
the news
away

THE TRAINEE

In London for a TEFL course,
Mike is being faithful

to his girl-friend in Japan.
They're linking up again next month.

Besides sincerity,
he's noted for his striking looks

and the class he's been assigned to teach
is full of flirtatious women

from Paris, Rome and Sao Paulo.
Our tutor, who observed him yesterday,

advised him that his lead-in was too slow
and the dream he had last night

has left him feeling stressed.
He dreamt he was standing facing his class

with an unpeeled banana in his fist.
I asked him what he thought that signified.

I'm sure, he said, *it represents
my slow lead-in. What else?*

THE AFFAIR

Daddy's back she said,
hearing the key in the lock.
*See if **he** likes it or not*

The heat-wave was wearing her out
but now she could have a rest.

Buttercup in fist,
the little boy rushed to the door.*

Don't do that! his father roared,
swiftly re-clothing his neck
with the scarf the kid had yanked.

She fanned her face
with a colouring-pad
and said, *Another sore throat?*

---

* A person's liking for butter can be measured by the strength of a buttercup's
reflection on the skin of the neck.

THE THAMES LINK

A couple and a male friend meet
on the Thames Link morning train.

Driven by the random thrust
of shoulders, elbows, knees,
a woman joins their ring,
creating the illusion of two pairs.

How's Rachel? asks the wife.
Rolling his eyes with a hoot,
the friend replies, *Don't ask!*
The husband sniggers, *Still in her own world?*

Meanwhile the stranger in the ring
is gazing absently ahead
at the silver sheets of mist
peeling off the Thames.

WEDNESDAY

after adjusting the pillow
under her back
a number of times

she asked him to withdraw
to put some music on

he fiddled with the switches
           & the knobs

to no avail
until she pointed out
that it wasn't turned on
at the mains

DELAYED

The Tube is congested again.
Waiting for my train,
I can barely free my wedged hand

to wipe my brow.
Lining the wall ahead,
behind the track,

the monumental image of a plug
pulled by a chain
out of its hole

confronts the crowd.
It's an advert for a laxative.
How long is this going to last?

THIRD WORLD RUINS

Through a window
of the museum,
where Roman pumps and taps
are on display,

I watch a woman climb
a steep hill,
towards a shack,
buckling under a Jerry-can.

DEPARTURE

Waiting, with impatience,
for this train to move.

At last, the whistle blows.

The window slides across
the windows of the train
that halted next to ours.

They start to blur.

But clearing the final coach
with climbing speed,

our train stops dead,

without the faintest jolt,

beside a vacant track
in the station.

DAILY BREAD

I liked him.
He was urbane,
Nonchalantly erudite
& wry.

He was in Euromoney,
My final port of call,
In which I had to rid myself
Of as many of my wares
As possible,

In order to cut my losses
Or make a pathetic
Profit.

He always had an Egg Mayonnaise sandwich
So I always reserved one for him,
Knowing it would go.

One day,
Despite reminding me
The day before
To save one for the morrow,
He wasn't there.

He'd been called away,
Minutes before my arrival,
On urgent personal business.

By leaving he had jettisoned
A hot deal in the making, I was told.

The following day
I was landed once again
With the sandwich I had saved for him

Because the afternoon before,
He'd thrown himself
Off the top floor
Of a council estate
In Pimlico,

A place with which
Nobody was the least aware
He had the slightest link.

Thereafter, if I reached
My final port of call
With an Egg Mayo sandwich
In my basket,
It would be by chance
Rather than design,

And sometimes it would go
And sometimes it wouldn't.

LIZ & RAY

last month when Liz & Ray came round
Liz, usually fairly prim,
arrived in a c thru leotard
and moved away each time
Ray tried to cuddle her

then she danced alone
in a way i'd never seen her dance
brandishing her pelvis
and strutting

and didn't I hear her extolling
the virtues of sharing & giving?

she said she'd met a band
and showed me a photo
of Steed, the vocalist,
caressing his loins
with a mike

that was last month

last night when they came round
Liz was dressed
in a bulky, nunnish skirt
and continually held Ray's hand

i can't remember her dancing once

but i do recall
she complained a lot
about a large sum of money

she'd lent to someone
and hadn't got back

ICE CREAM VAN

children and lovers queue
at the ice cream van

throbbing in the park.
the fridge, I imagine, is powered

by the van's engine
which is always left on.

you can see the emission,
a pulsing jet,

hammered out of the pipe
and skipping across the grass,

bending vision,

these sweltering afternoons
that foster trade

A FREE MOUSE

It's quite spacious - there are two floors.
A treading-wheel affords
a boundless run
or gallop, if you will.
Wedged between the bars, a notice says:

Cage supplied with a free mouse.

PHONE BOOTH

Inverted, as if mirrored,
when looked at from inside,

the lettering
in white metallic paint,

on the glass door,
is hard to read

against the solar glare.
But, standing in the trapped heat,

I read the shadow of **FIRE**
across my sleeve,

the right way round,
in carbon print.

MEMORY

When the alarm
drove a wedge

into the fontanelle
of his sleep,

he had to separate
his clothes from hers,

which lay discarded on the floor.
Once on the street,

which was still quiet
and still dark,

he looked for someone
to ask the way.

THE PRIVATE MAN

he never uses
a public toilet
one can never be sure
who's been using that seat...

and he never drinks
in a public house
one can never be sure
who's been using that glass...

a jingle announces his presence
his pockets
are full
of coins

but has he ever considered
whose hands these coins have passed through?

they've passed through the hands
of prostitutes, junkies,
carriers of disease,
immigrants,
beggars,
navvies
tramps

and all the scum of the earth

DISCONNECTION

As her eyes began to well,
She said the water man had been.

DECEMBER 94, LONDON

the heat kept me awake till dawn
when, just as I was drifting off,
that fly began to drone
and smack against the pane

another bright morning
another cloudless sky
the flowers in the park
are coming into bloom

beside the market-place
wagons of culled fir-trees
have suddenly appeared
and bird-song fills the air

BLACK & WHITE
(for Josephine)

Seven months after you were conceived,
On the day your aunt was cremated,
Your grandmother, clad in black, began
To knit a white dress for you.

WEDDING

all necks stretch
as the freshly wedded bride
kneels at the altar

revealing the price
of her shoes

YES, LOVE?

Standing with his back to the counter
while he waited to be served,
he ran his fingers through
his mass of tumbling curls.

Yes, love? the butcher cawed,
trying, but failing, to gain
his attention from behind.

Leaning forward,
he repeated the words,
raising his voice,
a gruff and hard-edged bass,

but the stranger, whose face
suggested a history of brawls,

remained unresponsive
until a person in the queue
informed him, with some diffidence,
that he was next.

THE LINGUIST

The woman who works in the library,
The one who never stops talking,
Told me she discovered
Her aptitude for languages
When she went on holiday to France once
And had the terrible experience
Of not being able to talk.

Now, armed with French,
Italian and Greek,
She can talk to her heart's content
From Aberdeen to Athens.
Turkey, you're next.

NOCTURNE

Sitting on the swing,
She started to have regrets.
Her frustration was understandable.
It was boring being married
To an unresponsive oaf.
But what she'd just done was dangerous.
She also began to consider
The value of the vase.

She walked back down the garden
And stood at the window-ledge.
Shrouded in night's ink,
She could see him clearly
In the starkly lit room.

He was on his knees on the floor,
His hair matted with blood,
Engrossed by the challenge
Of gluing together
The bits.

SUPPER

A vehemence locked
her tear-streaked jaw,
as she acted the incident out.

After a few rotations,
the bag she'd returned with
from the take away
began to blur
like the blades
of a propeller,

and I ducked to avoid the fate
her assailant had just met
on that badly lit stretch
of Coldharbour Lane.

When she finished,
she started crying again.

Didn't anyone try to help? I asked.

There was no one around! she sobbed.

I hugged her
and praised her indomitable spirit,
until she at last calmed down.

Then I dipped my hand
into the carrier-bag
and took out a pair of cartons.

Made of a kind of reinforced card,
they seemed quite tough and hard
and showed no sign of wear.

Weighing them in my hands,
I saw that they could fetch
a fairly fearsome smack.

I unclipped one
and considered the contents.

It looked okay.
It smelt okay.
Tasted okay as well

although, considering the stress
and friction it had undergone,
it was a bit cold.

OWN CLOTHES DAY

When she strode into the staff-room
Without the slightest diffidence,

Ralph pointed at the door
And ordered her to leave,

At which point recognition dawned.

Aside from his short-sightedness,
He had forgotten it was Own Clothes Day

When, as a playful foil
To pupils dressed informally,

Some staff dress in the pupils' uniform.

Ignoring his apologies,
The head approached
And briskly said, *A word.*

She forced an exhalation through
The red reed of her lips,

Before continuing.

You need, she said, *to cultivate
More strength and more authority*

To tacitly confound this claim,
Ralph looked her boldly in the eye

And strayed into acquaintance with
Her muddy irises,

While she listed the facets
Of human callousness
(Innate ability to spot
Weakness & so forth)

And toyed with a plat
That hung beside
The heraldry
Of her tie.

FRENCH

I made some flashcards
to model words that name
locations.

The first, a photo of a stadium,
elicited much strutting
and the chorus of

LE STUD!

The second showed
a Nat West branch,
and prompted the collective roar of

LA BONK!

I checked to see what the next one was.
It was the swimming-pool.

SETTING OFF

To avoid her ire,
I dropped the key
to quickly get a better grip.

We eased her drawings into the boot
and now there was nothing left to do
but drive way.
And we'd left ourselves enough time.
Hooray!

Cheerfully she put
her arms around my neck,

but as I enjoyed
the restorative warmth
of her clasp,
I felt the flatness
of my trouser-pockets
and noticed the bars

of a long, wide drain
underneath
our feet.

THE SEARCH

where's the corkscrew
i asked
thru the kitchen-wall
after a moment's search

silence

i rummaged
a bit more
& then gave up
& went in2
the adjacent room
where we'd been sitting

it appeared 2b
deserted

my instincts
became mobilised
as, rooted to the floor,
i checked
the cavity
beneath her desk

Then crept silently
2 the balcony
2c if I could spy
a loose helix
of gold
poking out of a crate

she'd vanished
& the silence
was profound

i tip-toed
2 the threshold
of her painting-space
& peeped in

the profoundest of silences!
not a stir!

but a corner was hidden
by the half-open door
i knew she was there!
it was the last place left!

with impish trepidation
i peeped
thru the hinge-crack
ready 2 surprise
& pounce
with a burst
of hilarity

& saw her,
oblivious of me,
her profile obscured
by that candelabra
of golden ringlets,

engrossed by a drawing
she'd been working on

and I went back 2 the kitchen
2 resume
my original
search

TRANSPARENCY

Before unlocking the door,
We had to do the dots.

I peeled one off the roll
But Victor delayed

The job's completion
With a long French kiss.

When I opened my eyes,
Bliss was dispelled

By horror. Through the glass front,
My eyes met my husband's eyes.

He was standing outside on the pavement.
He produced a knife.

With the white adhesive dot
Stuck to my fingertip,

I could only watch, appalled,
As he charged.

Lightning Source UK Ltd.
Milton Keynes UK
UKOW040643141112

202126UK00001B/28/P

9 781901 990034